Design and Make
TOYS THAT MOVE

Helen Greathead

A+

Smart Apple Media

Contents

Introduction

Moving toys have been around for much longer than you might think! The spinning top is one of the oldest toys. It's also one of the simplest to make.

Changing technology

Throughout history, as new technology has changed our way of life, toys have changed, too. Toy trains became popular soon after real trains were

invented in the 1800s. The first pull-along wooden trains came out in the 1840s. By the 1870s, tin-plate trains were powered by clockwork mechanisms or steam. By the end of the century, German toy companies were making train tracks and other accessories.

Building bricks

Frank Hornby started his toy-making business in 1901 after making a collection of metal bricks that connected together with nuts and bolts. The idea was to encourage his son's interest in engineering. The bricks caught on, and soon, more complex construction kits were on sale. Children could build a skyscraper, or even a ship or an airplane! Such kits are still highly popular with children today.

Fantastic plastic

World War II stopped toy production in many countries, since factories were needed to make weapons instead. In the United States, some toy factories stayed open, but toys were never quite the same! After the war, wood and tin plate were out, and plastic was in! Plastic was easy to mold, quick to produce, and cheap to buy.

Transforming toys

Toys then became more complex and exciting in the way they were made. The 1980s featured popular toys such as Transformers, which changed from things such as planes and cars into robots. These toys were simply a matter of clever mechanisms. Meanwhile, Japanese toy makers developed new ideas for toys that were battery-operated. Batteries had been used before to make sounds and flashing lights, but the new toys could now move, too.

Making toys

In this book, you can find out how to design and make your own moving toys. From a simple spinning top to a battery-operated alien, you can try your hand at making all kinds of mechanisms. Whichever toy projects you choose, you are likely to have fun designing and making them, as well as playing with them!

Be prepared

Here is a list of all the materials and equipment you will need to make the different toys in this book.

Hints and tips

* Always read the instructions completely through BEFORE you start.
* Clear plenty of space to work in.
* Always try laying things out before you put your model together.
* Take time to think about your ideas. If you get stuck, talk your problem through with a friend or an adult.

Things to collect

Hole punch

Bodkin

Needles and thread

Craft knife

Pencils and pens

Compass

Hacksaw

Dowels (wood and balsa wood) of various lengths and widths

Straws

Popsicle sticks

Boxes of all shapes and sizes

Old-fashioned clothespins

Ready-made wheels

Pipe-cleaners

Ricrac

Styrofoam balls

Self-hardening clay

Embroidery thread

Plastic cartons

Buttons

String

Plastic eyes

Felt-tip pens

Pom-poms

Shiny scraps of paper and fabric

Paints

Glow-in-the-dark paint

Netting—from bags of oranges, lemons, or onions

Beads

Feathers

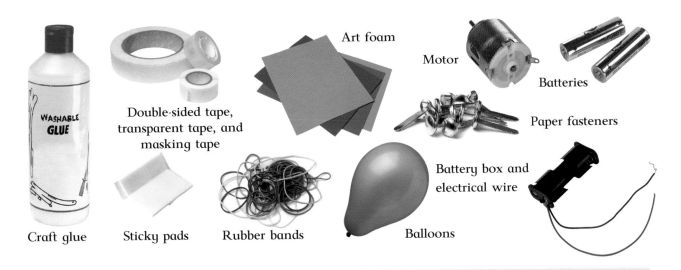

Art foam

Motor

Batteries

Paper fasteners

Double-sided tape, transparent tape, and masking tape

Battery box and electrical wire

Craft glue

Sticky pads

Rubber bands

Balloons

Wheels

✴ You can use all sorts of things for wheels. Collect old plastic lids, cartons, and cardboard tubes of different shapes and sizes and try them out.

✴ Ready-made wheels probably work best, though. You can find these at most craft stores.

✴ Dowels make ideal axles. Balsa dowels can be cut with a craft knife, but be careful—they break easily.

✴ Measure carefully to figure out where the holes for the axles should be. They will need to align on each side.

✴ Once the body of your vehicle is finished, attach the wheels to the dowel using strong glue. You might need to taper the dowel to fit. (Try using a pencil sharpener for wooden dowels.)

✴ Don't make the wheels fit too closely to the sides of your vehicle. Put a small disk between the wheel and the vehicle to help the wheels turn.

✴ String can also make a good axle if you tie it very tightly.

MAKING HOLES

✴ Make a very small hole to start with, and gradually make it bigger.

✴ Always check whether the hole you make needs to hold something firmly or to allow for some movement.

Spiral spinning top

Here's a simple moving toy that's easy to make.

Design and select

Make a simple spinning top with a spiral pattern. Choose your materials and sketch some ideas before you start. We used tagboard, a short pencil, a compass, and paint. You could use glow-in-the-dark paint to make the top extra special!

Make

1 Use a compass to draw a circle on a piece of brightly colored tagboard. Make a mark in the middle with the compass point. Carefully cut out the circle.

2 Decorate the circle with an interesting design using paint. Start at the center where you made your mark and work outward. Put it somewhere safe to dry.

Challenge

Try using different materials to make a top. What other shapes can you use?

3 Use a short pencil to make the shaft of the top.

Challenge
What else could you use for the shaft?

4 Carefully make a hole in the middle of the circle with the point of the pencil and push it through. The tagboard should just fit on the pencil. Don't push it up too high!

Challenge
Experiment to find the best position of the circle on the shaft. When does it spin the longest?

5 Find a large, flat, smooth surface. Turn out the lights and spin the top on the point of the pencil.

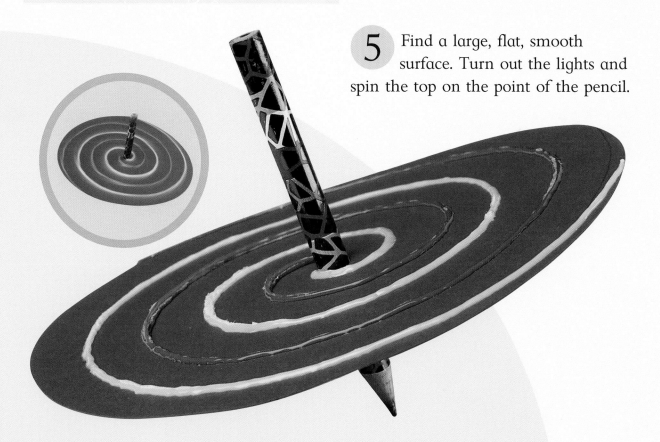

Pop-up surprise

This pop-up surprise is simple to make but very effective.

Design and select

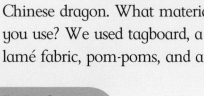

Make a colorful pop-up surprise. Look at pictures of animals or people and sketch some ideas. We've made a Chinese dragon. What materials will you use? We used tagboard, a cork, green lamé fabric, pom-poms, and a dowel.

Look at this!

Here's a colorful Chinese dragon to give you some inspiration! This one is used at the Chinese New Year.

✱ How do you think this dragon moves?

Make

1   Draw and cut out a semi-circle using a piece of tagboard. Cut some fabric about an inch (2.5 cm) larger than the tagboard and glue it onto one side, gluing the edges neatly on the other side. Using a dowel to determine the size, bend the tagboard into a cone and glue together, but don't glue it to the rod.

2   Cut a long strip of fabric the same length as the dowel rod. Sew it into a tube, right-sides together, leaving about 1.5 inches (4 cm) unstitched at one end. Turn the tube the right way out.

3   Push the dowel through the tube with the unstitched end at the bottom. Gather the top end of the tube and attach it to the dowel with tape.

10

4 At the other end of the fabric tube, cut some slits in the material. Push the cone you made earlier onto the end of the dowel rod and stick the material down inside the cone. Decorate the cone with ricrac.

5 Cut out a head and nose from shiny tagboard. Glue some cork on the face so that the nose juts out. Add a tongue, fur, and horns. Glue on small pom-poms for eyes.

Challenge
How else could you make the head more 3D?

6 Use sticky pads and double-sided tape to attach the head to the dowel rod, and bend a piece of tagboard for the back of the head (right). Make your creature pop up!

Hop-along hen

This hen looks almost real as it bobs up and down!

Design and select

Make a push-along bobbing bird for a toddler. Draw some bird sketches and think about which ones will work best. How can you decorate them? We used strong tagboard, paint, art foam, feathers, plastic eyes, and a balsa dowel rod.

Look at this!

This wooden toy duck clatters along as you push it.

✳ Why doesn't it have round wheels?

✳ Which part of the duck moves as it rolls along?

Make

1 Draw your bird on a piece of tagboard, cut out two shapes, and decorate one side of each piece. Make sure they are the opposite sides.

Challenge
What else could you use to make the body?

2 Make wheels from thick cardboard. Pierce a hole off-center with the tip of a pencil in the same place on both wheels. Paint them a bright color.

3 Ask an adult to help you make a hole through the balsa dowel, half an inch (1 cm) from the end (you can use a bodkin). Make a hole with a hole punch half an inch (1 cm) from the bottom of each hen, making sure they are in exactly the same position on each hen.

Challenge
Could you make a bird with wings that flap?

4 Thread some thick string through the balsa dowel and then through the holes in the hens, placing one on each side of the dowel. Add a wheel on each side and tie a knot in the string to hold them on securely.

5 Attach the hen pieces to the dowel with sticky pads and stick the hen together at the head and tail with more sticky pads. Glue on some feathers to make a tail. Push your hen along and watch it bob!

Challenge
Make your bird rattle as it rolls!

Sparkly mobile

Blow on this mobile and watch it move!

Look at this!

Alexander Calder made sculptures out of wire. He made some enormous mobiles! His sculptures are described as kinetic art, because they move.

✱ What materials do you think Calder used to make the fish?

✱ How did he attach the shapes?

Design and select

Design a fish mobile and decorate it with sparkly shapes. Sketch some designs for your fish shapes. How will the pieces of your mobile connect? We used pipe cleaners, wool, net (from a bag of oranges), plastic eyes, felt, and anything shiny!

Make

1 Bend and twist a pipe cleaner to make a fish shape. Make four shapes in all.

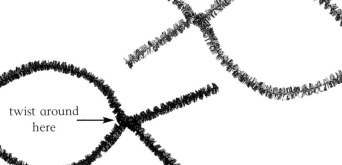

twist around here →

Challenge
What could you use instead of pipe cleaners?

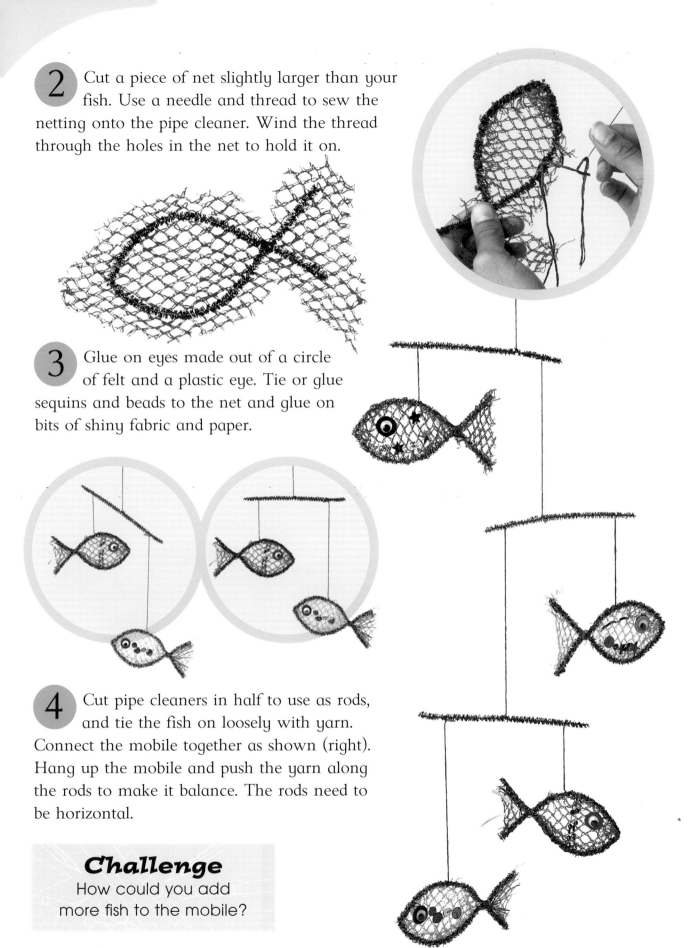

2 Cut a piece of net slightly larger than your fish. Use a needle and thread to sew the netting onto the pipe cleaner. Wind the thread through the holes in the net to hold it on.

3 Glue on eyes made out of a circle of felt and a plastic eye. Tie or glue sequins and beads to the net and glue on bits of shiny fabric and paper.

4 Cut pipe cleaners in half to use as rods, and tie the fish on loosely with yarn. Connect the mobile together as shown (right). Hang up the mobile and push the yarn along the rods to make it balance. The rods need to be horizontal.

Challenge
How could you add more fish to the mobile?

Lift-up ladder engine

Make a fire engine
that really works.

Design and select

Make a fire engine with a lift-up ladder
and a wind-up hose. Choose your materials.
We used a small cardboard box, ready-made
wheels, dowels, wooden popsicle sticks, paints,
a rubber band, a paper fastener, a pipe
cleaner, string, and a long balloon.

Make

1 Cut the top off your box and give it a coating
of red paint—the open side of the box will
be the bottom of your engine. Make four holes for
the wheels using your ready-made wheels and
a ruler to determine how high up they
should be. The guidelines (right) show
where to place your wheels.

2 To make the ladder rungs, ask an adult to help
you cut popsicle sticks in half with scissors. Glue the
rungs onto four uncut sticks to make the ladder—it needs
to be the same length as your box. Paint the ladder silver.

3 Use a craft knife to make two holes for the ladder in the roof (left). The front hole needs to be long and as wide as the square dowel (see step 5).

4 Tie a rubber band around the second rung of the ladder. Push the band through the smaller hole. Wrap the other end of the rubber band around a small piece of dowel to hold it loosely in place (right).

5 To lift the ladder, you need a lever. Ask an adult to help you make this by cutting two pieces of square dowel. One should be 1.5 inches (4 cm) wider than the box; the other should be two-thirds of the height of the box. Tape the pieces together to form a T-shape, with the longer piece forming the top of the T. Paint the T silver.

6 Ask for help to make a slit in each side of the box so that the lever can move up and down. Add a notch at the top to hold the lever in place, as shown below. Figure out the curve of the slit with a compass, starting one-third of the way up the box, as shown at right.

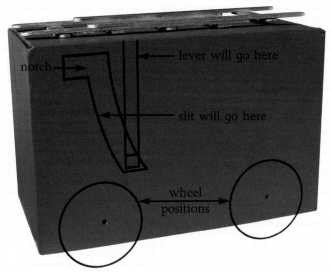

notch
lever will go here
slit will go here
wheel positions

7 Push the lever inside the box and poke the ends out of the slits on each side. Tape the central bar of the lever onto the ladder through the large hole in the top of the box. Move the lever to work the ladder.

Challenge
How could you add a roll-up door?

continued ⟶

8 To make the wind-up hose, cut two disks of tagboard two inches (5 cm) in diameter and paint them black. Attach one to the end of your engine with a paper fastener. Cut a one-inch (2.5 cm) strip from a narrow cardboard tube and glue it to the center of the other disk. Make a hole in the disk inside the cardboard tube.

Disc

Cardboard tube

9 Cut a piece of pipe cleaner about two inches (5 cm) long and push it through the hole you just made. Tape the end down securely on the inside of the cardboard tube. Fold the other end of the pipe cleaner over to make a handle. Glue the tube onto the disk you fastened to the engine. The cross-section picture, right, shows you how all the sections connect. Now, glue on a long balloon to make the hose.

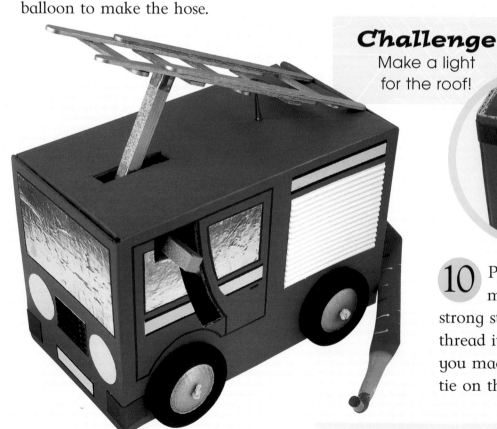

Challenge
Make a light for the roof!

10 Paint your ready-made wheels. Use strong string for the axles, thread it through the holes you made in step 1, and tie on the wheels.

11 Add more decoration to your engine, such as windows and doors. Now it's ready to roll!

Challenge
Use some of these techniques to make a digger that lifts up its loader.

Shark shock

This toy uses a cam mechanism to make it bob up and down.

Design and select

Use a cam mechanism to make a shark shoot out of the sea! Think about the look of your shark (look at some photographs) and sketch your ideas. What materials will you use? We used strong cardboard, wooden dowels, art foam, sticky pads, and plastic eyes.

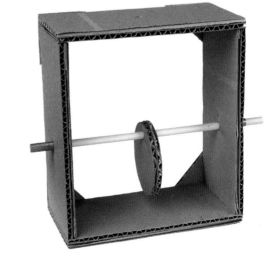

Look at this!

Turn the handle on this machine and the boat sinks, then rises again.

* What is it made from?

* How do you think the cat moves?

Make

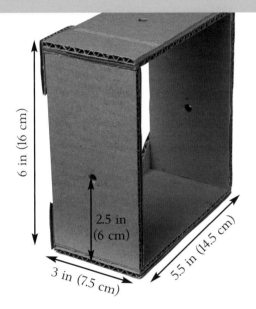

6 in (16 cm)

2.5 in (6 cm)

3 in (7.5 cm)

5.5 in (14.5 cm)

1 Make a box from strong cardboard 5.5 inches (14.5 cm) wide by 6 inches (16 cm) high by 3 inches (7.5 cm) deep. Add triangular supports at each corner on the back (shown right). With a pencil, pierce a small hole in the center of the top and one in each side, 2.5 inches (6 cm) up from the bottom.

2 Get help to cut a piece of dowel eight inches (20 cm) long with a hacksaw. Cut out a disk of cardboard with a 2.5-inch (6 cm) diameter and make a hole in it off-center. Now, push the dowel through one of the holes on the side, through the hole in the disk, and then through the hole in the other side of the box. Wind some tape around each end of the dowel to hold it in place.

19

3 Cut out another disk of cardboard 2.5 inches (6 cm) in diameter and make a hole in its center. Cut a piece of dowel the same height as the box. Push this through the hole in the top of the box and glue the disk on its bottom.

4 To make a handle for your machine, cut out a rectangle of cardboard 1 inch (2.5 cm) by 1.5 inches (4 cm) and make two holes in it. Cut a piece of dowel 1.2 inches (3 cm) long and push it through one hole of the rectangle. Push the other end onto the horizontal dowel, as shown below.

5 To make the shark, fold a piece of art foam in half, draw half a shark shape, and cut it out carefully.

6 Use sticky pads to stick the sides of the shark together at the front and back. Don't fold the tail over, but make a slit in it so that it will stick up. Make slits for the gills and add plastic eyes. Glue the shark in position on the vertical dowel.

Challenge
Add another cam to make a swimmer bob up and down in the water!

7 Cut and decorate some paper to look like the sea and glue it on the front. Turn the handle and watch out for the shark!

21

Balloon racing car

Blow up the balloon and
watch this car go!

Look at this!

This car is made out
of plastic and can
move fast.

✽ Why do you
think the balloon
makes the car move?

✽ Why do you
think the car is
made of plastic?

Design and select

Make a racing car that is powered by an ordinary balloon!
Choose your materials and sketch out your ideas. Remember
that this car needs to be very light. We made the car using art
foam, straws, a balloon, cardboard, and sticky pads.

Make

1 Cut out a rectangle of
foam; lightly score a line
lengthwise down the middle with a
craft knife. Fold it in half. Draw the
shape of half of your racing car, with the
top of the car on the fold, and cut
it out carefully. Make holes in
the sides for the axles. Stick
the foam together at
the front with a
sticky pad.

2 Make the wheels out of four circles of cardboard, making two of them slightly smaller for the front wheels. Cut them out and paint them black and silver.

3 Cut pieces of straw for the axles and slot them through the holes in the sides of the car. Add a dab of glue onto the ends of the straw and stick on the wheels.

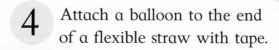

4 Attach a balloon to the end of a flexible straw with tape.

Challenge
Try putting the balloon in different positions to see if it still works.

5 Slot the straw underneath the foam body of the car above the axles with the balloon at the front. Secure the end with tape.

6 Blow through the straw to inflate the balloon. Quickly put the car on a smooth surface and watch it whiz away! (If your car stops working, try changing the balloon.)

Challenge
Can you decorate the car without making it too heavy?

Roll-along monster

This monster's mood
changes as it rolls along!

Design and select

Design a moving monster powered by a rubber band!
Sketch different facial expressions first, then choose your
materials. We used tagboard, a strong rubber band, two
straws, and some wooden dowels.

Make

1 To make a spool, cut a length of
cardboard tube slightly wider
than your rubber band. Cut two
tagboard disks for the ends with a
diameter about twice the size of the
tube. Use a pencil to make holes in
their centers big enough for a straw
to go through.

2 Attach the disks to
the tube with either
glue or tape.

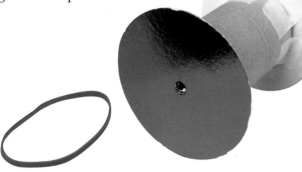

3 Cut a piece from a thick straw just longer
than the spool. Push it through the hole in
one disk and out the hole on the other side of the
spool. Make the straw stick out farther on one side.

4 Make a hook from a paper clip and use it to thread the rubber band through the straw. Use a small piece of dowel to hold the band on one side of the spool. Pull the band tight and tape down the dowel.

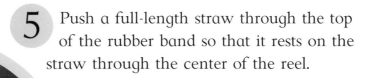

5 Push a full-length straw through the top of the rubber band so that it rests on the straw through the center of the reel.

6 Measure a strip of paper to wrap around the tube. Create two different faces on the strip, one above the other—one happy, one angry. Attach it to the spool.

Challenge
How could you make a hat for the monster? Where would you have to attach it?

7 Wind the long straw around and around until you can feel the rubber band tightening. Put the monster on a smooth surface and watch it roll toward you!

Challenge
Try making moving monsters from lots of different containers.

Rapunzel's wind-up prince

Rapunzel lived in a tall tower, and a prince climbed up her braid to visit her. Make life easier for Rapunzel and pull the prince up for her!

Design and select

Make a tower with a pulley to lift Rapunzel's hair. Sketch some pictures to plan how the pulley will work. We used a cereal box, balsa dowels, waxed linen thread, a plastic cup, old-fashioned wooden clothespins, felt, paint, embroidery thread, pipe cleaners, felt-tip pens, and plastic eyes.

Make

1 Cut off a section of a cereal box about two-thirds of its width. Make a slit in the side near the top and push in half a plastic cup to make the balcony. Tape the cup down at the sides. Give the tower and balcony a coating of paint.

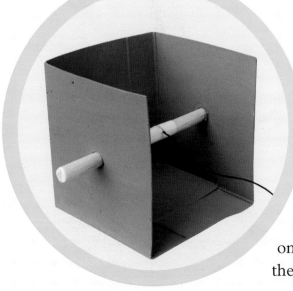

2 Cut off a corner from the leftover cereal box and paint it the same color as the tower. Make holes through its sides and push a piece of dowel about four inches (10 cm) long through the holes. This is your pulley. Tape one end of a piece of waxed thread 20 inches (50 cm) long to the center of the dowel. Tape or glue the pulley on top of the tower with the open part facing the front (see page 27).

3 Make clothespin dolls for Rapunzel and the prince. Glue pipe cleaners onto the pegs for arms and make simple outfits out of felt. Draw faces with felt-tip pens and glue on plastic eyes. Braid some embroidery thread to make Rapunzel's hair. It should be a little longer than the cereal box. Glue it onto her head.

Challenge
How could you make the witch in the story pop up in the tower?

4 Set Rapunzel in the tower and weave the loose end of the waxed thread through her braid. Wrap the prince's arms around the braid (right) and tie securely with thread.

Challenge
How could you pull the prince up using a motor?

5 Make a turret roof from a semi-circle of tagboard (see page 10) and set it on top of the tower. Paint bricks and windows. Turn the pulley to pull up the prince!

27

Battery-operated alien

Press a switch to make the alien dizzy!

Design and select

Make a toy alien, using a battery-operated circuit to spin its head around. Think about your design and sketch some ideas. Choose your materials. We've used a styrofoam ball, a yogurt container, and some clay. You will also need some batteries, a battery box, electrical wire, paper fasteners, cardboard, paint, and a small motor.

Make

1 Cut out a large circle of cardboard for the circuit base.

2 Your battery box will probably have two wires attached to it. Ask for help to strip off the plastic on the ends of the wires. Attach one of the wires to the motor, twisting it around the hooks as shown at right. Attach another wire to the other side of the motor.

3 Cut a small hole in the bottom of the yogurt container. Push the top of the motor through the hole and secure it inside the container with clay.

4 Make a switch from a folded square of cardboard with a paper fastener pushed through each side. Make sure the heads of the paper fasteners are on the inside of the switch and that they touch when you fold it closed.

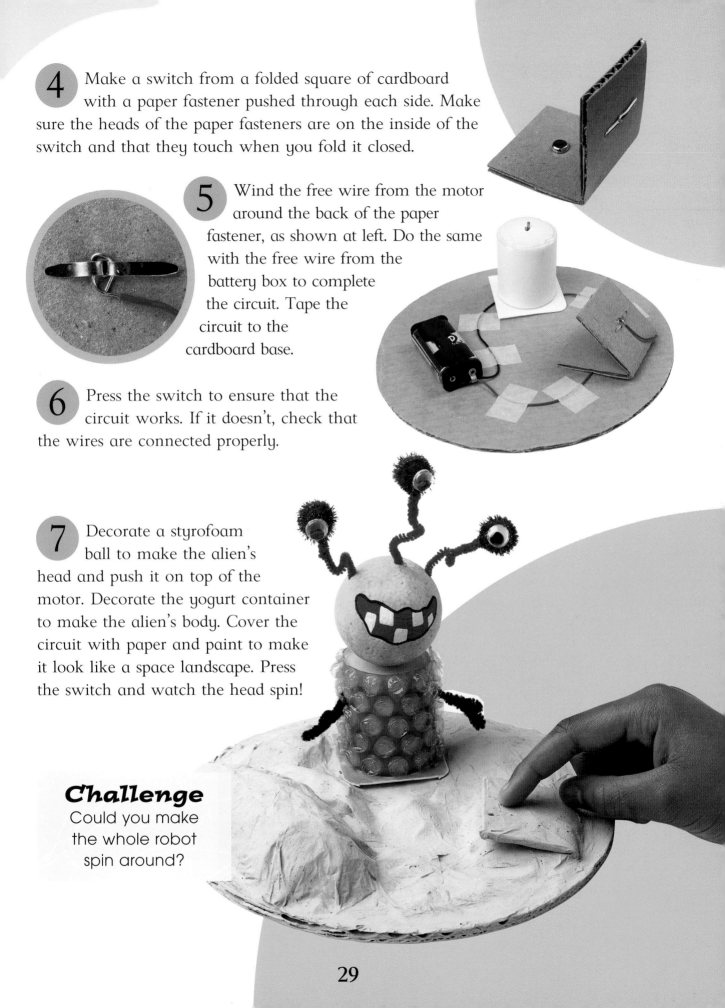

5 Wind the free wire from the motor around the back of the paper fastener, as shown at left. Do the same with the free wire from the battery box to complete the circuit. Tape the circuit to the cardboard base.

6 Press the switch to ensure that the circuit works. If it doesn't, check that the wires are connected properly.

7 Decorate a styrofoam ball to make the alien's head and push it on top of the motor. Decorate the yogurt container to make the alien's body. Cover the circuit with paper and paint to make it look like a space landscape. Press the switch and watch the head spin!

Challenge
Could you make the whole robot spin around?

29

Glossary

adhesive
something that makes things stick

aligned
to put things into a straight line
or in line with each other

axle
a bar or rod on which a wheel
or set of wheels turns

balsa wood
lightweight wood used to make model
boats and airplanes

bodkin
a blunt, thick needle used to thread
elastic or tape

cam
a projecting part on a rotating wheel
that makes another part move

dowels
thin, wooden rods

kinetic
having to do with or produced by
movement

lamé
material that has a shiny coating

lever
a handle used to operate or control
a piece of machinery

mechanism
the moving parts of a machine

notch
a small cut in a surface or on
the edge of something

pulley
a wheel with a grooved rim in which
a pulled rope or chain can run

right-sides
the side of the material that you
want to show

taper
to become gradually narrower
or thinner toward one end

Further information

You might find these Web sites helpful for finding ideas, techniques, and materials:

www.historychannel.com/ exhibits/toys/chess.html
A timeline of toys through the ages.

www.nga.gov/exhibitions/calder/ realsp/room11-10.htm
A virtual tour of an exhibition of Alexander Calder's work.

www.enchantedlearning.com/ crafts/mobiles
More ideas for mobiles you can make.

www.howstuffworks.com
More information about the mechanisms used in this book.

www.balloonhq.com/balloon_ car/balloon_car.html
Check out this site for some brilliant model balloon cars, including pictures and descriptions of how they were made.

http://storypalace.ourfamily.com/ c98B23.html
This site includes the story of Rapunzel.

http://automata.co.uk/gallery.htm
More ideas for how to use cam mechanisms.

www.walterruffler.de/ Designs.html
This site shows 25 cam models made out of paper.

www.nyu.edu/pages/ linguistics/courses/v610051/ gelmanr/
A gallery of historical automata.

www.mos.org/sln/Leonardo/ LeosMysteriousMachinery.html
Look at some of the amazing machines invented by Leonardo Da Vinci, then try to figure out what they were used for!

www.technologystudent.com/ cams/cam2.htm
See an example of a working cam.

Every effort has been made by the publishers to ensure that these Web sites are suitable for children, and contain no inappropriate or offensive material. However, because of the nature of the Internet, it is impossible to guarantee that the contents of these sites will not be altered. We strongly advise that Internet access is supervised by a responsible adult.

Index

First published in 2005 by
Franklin Watts, 96 Leonard Street
London EC2A 4XD

Franklin Watts Australia
Level 17/207 Kent Street, Sydney, NSW 2000

This edition published under license from Franklin Watts. All rights reserved.

Copyright © 2005 Franklin Watts

Editor: Rachel Tonkin; **Art Director:** Jonathan Hair;
Design: Matthew Lilly and Anna-Marie D'Cruz; **Photography:** Steve Shott.
Picture credits: Comstock Images/Alamy: 4c. © Dig. Image MoMA, New York/Scala. © 2005 DACS
London & ARS New York: 14t. Stock Connection Distribution/Alamy: 10t.
The publishers wish to thank Keith Newstead for permission to use the picture on page 19.
The author wishes to thank Patricia Greathead, Laurie Greathead, Angus McCubbine, and
Sacha Baker.

Published in the United States by Smart Apple Media
2140 Howard Drive West, North Mankato, Minnesota 56003

U.S. publication copyright © 2007 Smart Apple Media
International copyright reserved in all countries. No part of this book may
be reproduced in any form without written permission from the publisher.
Printed in the United States of America

Library of Congress Cataloging-in-Publication Data

Greathead, Helen.
Toys that move / by Helen Greathead.
p. cm. – (Design and make)
ISBN-13 : 978-1-58340-951-0
1. Toy making–Juvenile literature. 2. Mechanical toys–Juvenile literature.
I. Title. II. Design and make (North Mankato, Minn.)

TT174.G68 2006
745.592–dc22   2005051735

2 4 6 8 9 7 5 3 1